I0814617

Saiga Antelope

by Julie Murray

Abdo Kids Jumbo is an Imprint of Abdo Kids
abdobooks.com

abdobooks.com

Published by Abdo Kids, a division of ABDO, P.O. Box 398166, Minneapolis, Minnesota 55439.

Printed in the United States of America, North Mankato, Minnesota.

102024

012025

Photo Credits: Alamy, Minden Pictures, Shutterstock

Production Contributors: Teddy Borth, Jennie Forsberg, Grace Hansen
Design Contributors: Victoria Bates, Candice Keimig

Library of Congress Control Number: 2024936620

Publisher's Cataloging-in-Publication Data

Names: Murray, Julie, author.

Title: Saiga antelope / by Julie Murray

Description: Minneapolis, Minnesota : Abdo Kids, 2025 | Series: Unusual animals | Includes online resources and index.

Identifiers: ISBN 9798384903062 (lib. bdg.) | ISBN 9798384903765 (ebook) | ISBN 9798384904113 (Read-to-me ebook)

Subjects: LCSH: Antelopes--Juvenile literature. | Herbivores--Juvenile literature. | Hoofed animals--Juvenile literature. | Steppe animals--Juvenile literature. | Wildlife--Juvenile literature. | Enigmas--Juvenile literature.

Classification: DDC 599.646--dc23

Table of Contents

Saiga Antelope. 4

Body 10

Food 18

Baby Saiga Antelope. 20

More Facts 22

Glossary 23

Index 24

Abdo Kids Code. 24

Saiga Antelope

Saiga antelope have been around since the last **ice age**. They are found in central Asia. They live in open, dry **steppe** and semi-arid deserts.

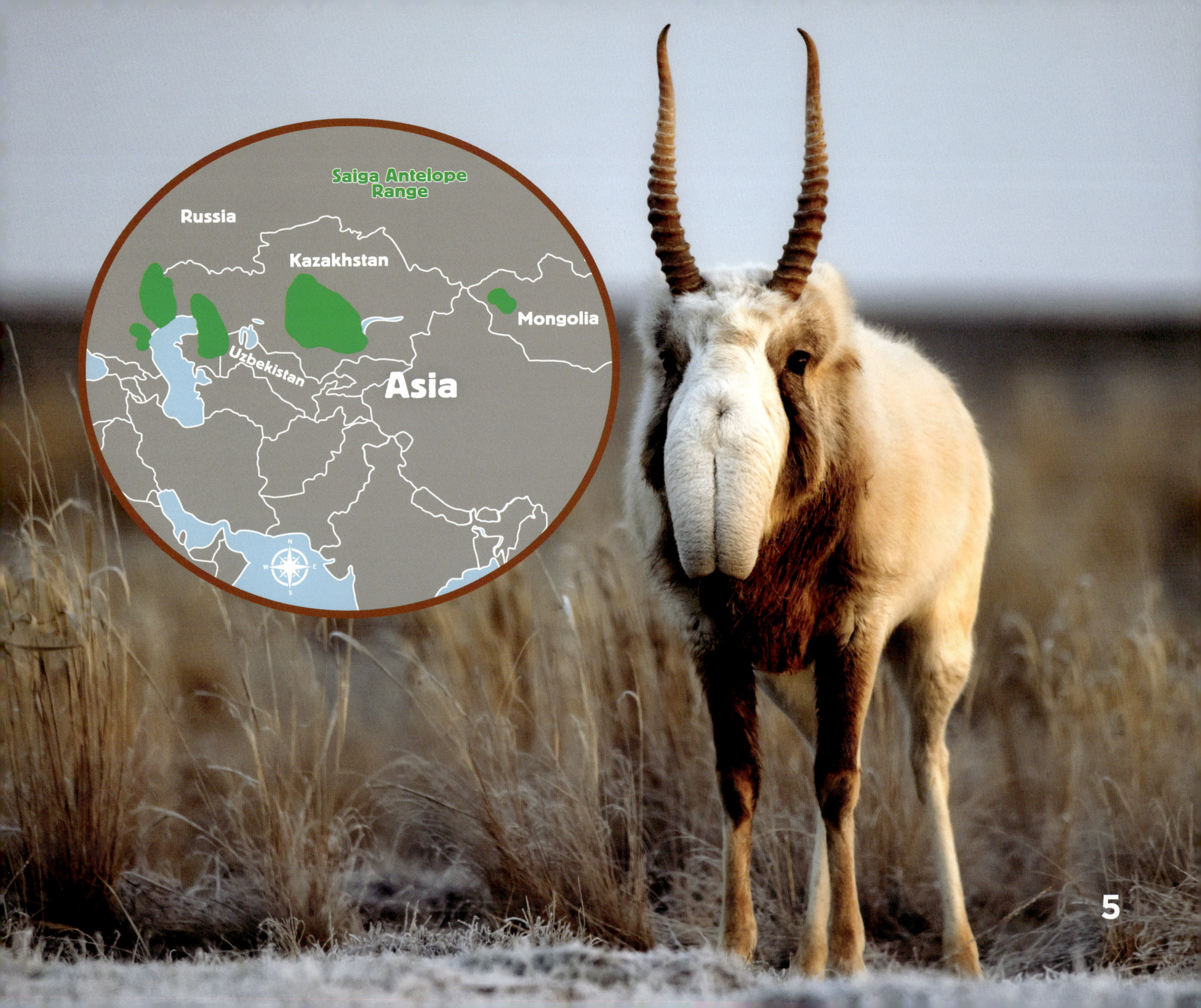
Saiga Antelope Range
Russia
Kazakhstan
Mongolia
Uzbekistan
Asia

The saiga antelope is an unusual animal. It has a very strange-looking face. Its large nose makes it look like a camel.

Camel

It is a **migratory** animal. It travels 600 miles (965 km) between the summer and winter months.

Body

Male saiga antelope stand around 2.5 feet (0.8 m) tall and 5 feet (1.5 m) long. They can weigh up to 150 pounds (68 kg). Females are smaller than males.

Saiga antelope have wool-like fur. The fur is tan with a creamy white underbelly. It grows thicker, longer, and lighter in color during the winter months.

Males have two horns on their heads. The horns have ring-like ridges around them. They can grow up to 10 inches (25 cm) long.

The saiga antelope's large nose is lined with **mucous membranes**. It filters out dust during the dry summers. It also warms up cold air in the winter. Males also use their nose to impress females.

Food

Saiga antelope are **herbivores**. They eat grasses, **lichens**, shrubs, and other plants. They eat many plants that are poisonous to other animals.

Baby Saiga Antelope

Females come together in the spring to give birth. About two-thirds give birth to twins. The others have a single calf. Babies drink their mother's milk for their first four months of life.

More Facts

- Saiga antelope have been hunted for their meat, skin, and horns. Their horns are used in Chinese medicine.
- In 2015, more than 75% of the saiga population died from disease. Today, they are making a comeback with a population of more than 1 million.
- A saiga can run up to 50 miles per hour (80 kph)!

Glossary

herbivore – an animal that only feeds on plants.

ice age – a long period of time when glaciers covered large parts of the earth. The last ice age occurred between about 120,000 and 11,500 years ago.

lichen – a living thing that is a fungus and a form of algae or special bacteria living together.

migratory – of or pertaining to migration or an act of migrating.

mucous membrane – the moist, inner lining of some body cavities (such as the nose and mouth).

steppe – a broad, somewhat arid grass plain, especially the great plains in southeast Russia and southwest Asia.

Index

Asia 4

coloring 12

face 6

food 18, 20

fur 12

habitat 4

horns 14

migration 8

nose 6, 16

size 10

young 20

Visit **abdokids.com** to access crafts, games, videos, and more!

Use Abdo Kids code **USK3062** or scan this QR code!